Institute of Education • University of London

Learning, context and the role of technology

Rosemary Luckin

Professor of Learner Centred Design

Based on an Inaugural Professorial Lecture delivered at the Institute of Education, University of London, on 27 January 2009

Professor Rosemary Luckin

Learning, context and the role of technology

Introduction and theoretical grounding

The question at the heart of this talk is: how can we understand the concept of *context* in a way that will enable us to develop, deploy and evaluate technology effectively to help learners and those who are helping them to adapt the resources they find within a particular context to best support their learning needs? There is nothing new about the suggestion that one should explore the situation in which learning takes place in order to understand more about how we support learning (see for example Mercer, 1992, and Wood, Underwood and Avis, 1999). However, the models of context that might effectively support the development of technology-rich learning do not yet exist. There is much research from a wealth of different disciplines (for example, Dey, 2001; Rogers, 2006; Cole, 2003; and Nardi, 1996) that is relevant to this enterprise and needs to be integrated and synthesised to form such a model. These foundations are important, but are beyond the scope of this lecture. Here I want to focus upon a personal empirical journey that has influenced my own attempts to construct a useful model of learning context: a model that can offer a translation of theory into an abstract representation that can be shared amongst practitioners, technologists and beneficiaries as they explore how to realise the potential benefits afforded by the wide range of increasingly available technologies.

The model is grounded in the sociocultural principle that an individual's development is an interaction between that individual and her social and cultural environment. In particular, it has been influenced by Vygotsky's Zone of Proximal Development (ZPD) (1978, 1986). This defines an important role for those who are responsible for providing environments for learning and for those who play the role of a learner's More Able Partner (MAP), such as teachers, parents and peers. I interpret Vygotsky's ZPD through two additional concepts: the Zone of Available Assistance (ZAA) and the Zone of Proximal Adjustment (ZPA), as illustrated in Figure 1. The ZAA describes the variety of qualities and quantities of assistance that need to be available to enable the MAP to offer appropriate assistance to the child. The ZPA represents a selection from the ZAA appropriate for the given learner and educational situation. The goal for the MAPs and those developing technologies is to provide an appropriate range of resources within an environment and to engender effective negotiations between learner and MAPs to support an optimal ZPA from amongst these.

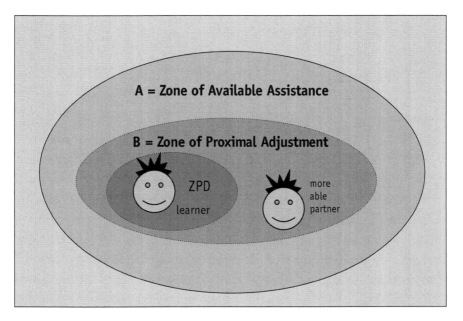

Figure 1 A graphical representation of the ZAA, ZPA and ZPD concepts

Building a model of a learner's context

I now concentrate upon how these theoretical foundations can be combined with evidence from empirical studies that have explored the role of technology to support learning. In my early work (Luckin, 1998; Luckin and du Boulay, 1999) I explored how the ZPD could inform software design and I developed the Ecolab software versions I and II as a research tool. The Ecolab software provided 10- to 11-year-old children with a simulated ecology laboratory environment and an artificial collaborative learning partner that offered adaptive assistance, or scaffolding (Wood *et al.*, 1976), based on a detailed student model. The software was designed for a single learner to use on a laptop or desktop computer, needing no connectivity beyond this machine. It involved modelling the learner and scaffolding her interactions. Initially, scaffolding in the Ecolab I software was designed with respect to a small curriculum of domain knowledge to be learnt. In the Ecolab II software, scaffolding was extended with respect to metacognition in terms of learners' help-seeking and learners' task selection.

The original Ecolab I software

The original Ecolab system (Luckin and du Boulay, 1999) was a software environment into which a child could place different organisms and with which she could explore the relationships that existed between them. The overall motivation presented to her was that she should explore which sort of organisms can live together and form a food web.

The Ecolab operated in two modes: 'build', which allowed the child to construct her mini world of plants and animals by adding those of her choice; and 'run', which enabled her to activate these organisms. If the child selected an action that was not possible she would be guided towards a possible alteration so that the effects of the selected action could be completed. The child controlled the software through mouse-driven commands selected from a series of menus.

The full complexity of the relationships between the Ecolab organisms was not offered to a new learner straight away, but could be introduced through

3

four phases of relationship complexity. In each of these phases the action commands available to the learner were appropriate to the complexity of the relationships that could be simulated in the Ecolab. For example, in phase one, which reflected the simplest situation, the relationships that the child could explore were those between an animal and the food that it eats. The commands available were therefore the 'eat' and 'eaten by' commands. The second phase of complexity allowed the formation of food chains, the third and fourth phases allowed the formation of food webs and relationships between all the different members of the web. The system could switch between these four phases from the less to the more complex, or in reverse from the more to the less complex. The terminology used to identify the organisms could also be varied. For example, whilst initially the child might be working out what happens to the energy level of a 'thrush' when it eats a 'snail', this may become an 'omnivore' eating a 'herbivore' or a 'secondary consumer' eating a 'primary consumer'.

Finally, the child could view the Ecolab simulation that she was building and activating from different perspectives as described below and as illustrated in Figure 2.

1   World view: a picture of the organisms selected by the child.
2   Web view: a diagrammatic representation of the organisms and the links between them in the style of a food web diagram as used in textbooks.
3   Energy view: a block graph illustrating each of the organisms in the Ecolab simulation in terms of their current level of energy.
4   History view: a textual description of what has happened in the Ecolab simulation to date.
5   Log view: a log that summarises all that has happened along with the current state of the simulation.

Within each of these views most of the screen objects would provide the child with information when clicked on with the mouse. For example, clicking on an organism in 'World view' would yield the organism's name, what it eats and what eats it. The choice of view used was largely, though not completely, under the child's control.

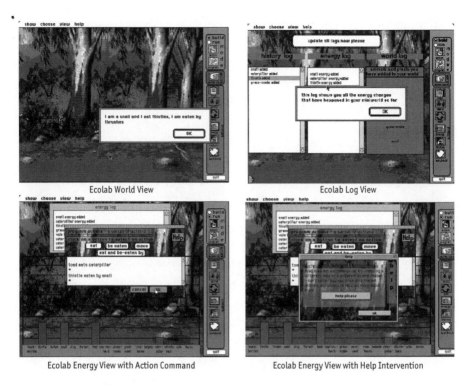

Figure 2 Some different views of the Ecolab 1 software

The Ecolab as a More Able Partner

In addition to this variably complex simulation that the child could build and activate, the Ecolab I software acted in the role of the MAP and could offer the child assistance or collaborative support in two main ways:

1 Through five levels of graded help specific to the particular situation. The higher the level of help the simpler the action required by the child and the greater the control taken by the system, resulting in there being less scope for the child to fail (Wood *et al.*, 1978).
2 Through the difficulty level of the activities the child was asked to complete using the Ecolab I software. There were 144 individual activities that could

be offered to the child. Three levels of Activity Differentiation were possible, from 0 (the hardest) to 2 (the easiest).

The Ecolab's knowledge about food chains and webs

In order to support the flexible complexity of the simulation environment and the provision of collaborative support, the Ecolab software needed a representation of the knowledge about food chains and webs it was helping the child to learn. The structure of the content knowledge representation in the Ecolab software was informed by the curriculum and by work done by educators who had identified particular difficulties that learners faced and who had made suggestions for the order in which concepts should be introduced (Griffiths and Grant, 1985; Lumpe and Staver, 1995, for example). The knowledge was represented as a system of rules that the child needed to understand if she was to understand the relationships that existed between the animals and plants in her simulation. The rules were grouped to correspond with the four phases of complexity of the Ecolab simulation. Each of these phases was associated with a subset of actions made available through the menu commands of the software. Each of the activities that a child could be asked to complete was associated with one of the rule nodes. The activities at any rule node could be offered at any of the three levels of Activity Differentiation.

The Ecolab's knowledge about the learner

The final component that enabled the Ecolab software to operate in the manner described was the model that the system built of the learner who was interacting with it. This was needed by the system in order to enable it to make decisions about the level of simulation complexity at which the Ecolab software should operate, the nature of the activity, its level of difficulty and the amount of support that the system would need to provide in order to ensure that the learner was successful when interacting at a node. For each learner who used the Ecolab I software, a model of the knowledge structure of rule and concept nodes was created. This was used to maintain a dynamic model of the learner's progress based upon her successful completion of activities and the amount of assistance she had used. A key point of progress was the realisation that to base a system upon an interpretation of the ZPD theory required finding a way to quantify how much help had been given to the learner.

Learning with and from the Ecolab I software

In evaluations of the Ecolab I software with a class of 30 primary school children aged 10 and 11 years all but one child demonstrated an increase in score between a pre-system-use test and a post-system-use test. The mean test scores for the class are illustrated in Figure 3.

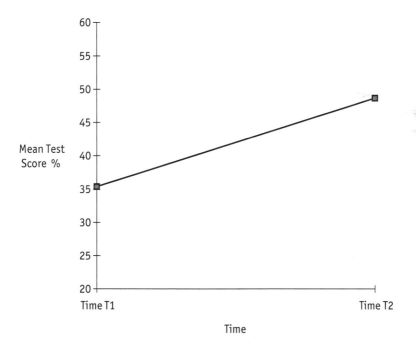

Figure 3 Ecolab I Mean Test Score by Time interaction

In addition to this type of quantitative analysis based on learning gains, each child's interactions with the Ecolab I software were logged. For each child a summary record of her interactions was produced from these logs so that the features of the software that the child actually used could be evaluated, as could any relationship between these and any gains in learning as recorded by the post-test. It was interesting to note that the children who achieved above average learning gains when using the Ecolab I software were from across the ability range and that the following common features were found in their interactions:

- 85 per cent interacted with the Ecolab I software in more than one phase of relationship *complexity*;
- 92 per cent used a high level of system *help* and/or a high level of *Activity Differentiation* and 76 per cent used an above average amount of help and/ or an above average amount of Activity Differentiation;
- 69 per cent had *both* interacted with more than one phase of Ecolab I complexity and had used above average levels and amounts of help and/or Activity Differentiation.

A full analysis of the Ecolab I data can be found in Luckin (1998).

The ZAA and ZPA in the Ecolab I

In the Ecolab I software the resources available to the learner (ZAA) were those within the software itself: the animals and plants that could be placed in the child's simulated world, the flexible complexity of the different phases of the simulation environment, the actions that could be completed and the different views that the child could use to look at her simulation. The underlying knowledge about food chains and webs used by the software was organised in a manner that reflected beliefs amongst educators about what were the required concepts to be learnt and which might be particularly problematic. This was in effect the curriculum to be studied through the child's interactions with

Ecolab I. The MAP was also embodied within the software through the manner in which the learner was offered different levels of help and activities at different levels of difficulty. Decisions about how to target the assistance offered by the MAP were based upon a detailed, dynamic model of 'beliefs' about the learner's ability to solve problems based upon the rules in the curriculum, and the amount of assistance she would need from the system in order to achieve success.

The way in which the assistance available within the Ecolab I software, the Ecolab ZAA, could be targeted for a particular learner to form her ZPA was through the software scaffolding techniques. The elements of the software context with which the learner could interact are illustrated in Figure 4.

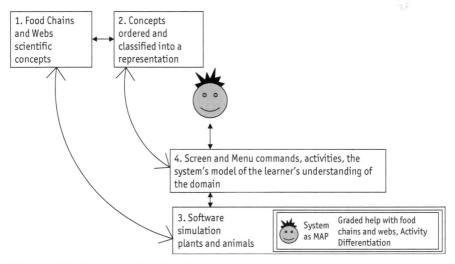

Figure 4 The Elements of the Ecolab I software context

The arrows in Figure 4 represent an *influences* relationship. The domain knowledge about food chains and webs represented as box 1 in Figure 4 has been organised into a particular representation *influenced by* prevalent beliefs about how the concepts should be taught and assessed. This organisation is described by box 2 in Figure 4. The arrow between boxes 1 and 2 indicates that the organisation of the scientific concepts into the Ecolab I knowledge representation, or curriculum, influences and has an impact upon the manner in which that information is structured. It does not, however, alter the nature of the underlying scientific concepts themselves, so the power of influence from box 2 to box 1 is weak here and the arrow connecting the two points is only in the direction from box 1 to box 2. Of course with more advanced learning interactions then it may well be that through such an organisation new knowledge about the underlying concepts might be gained. This would warrant a double-headed arrow indicating a bi-directional influential relationship between 1: subject knowledge, and 2: validation and organisation of subject knowledge into a curriculum.

The simulation offered to the learner in the Ecolab I software is represented in Figure 4 by box 3. As is clear from my earlier descriptions of the Ecolab I simulation, the features that the software offers are dependent upon the scientific concepts to be learnt, and their organisation into a curriculum, hence the link between box 3 and box 1. The manner in which the learner interacts with the curriculum and the scientific concepts to be learnt in this example is purely through the software. These interactions are administered through the interface and in particular through the menu commands and activities available to the learner, hence the link between box 3 and box 4 in Figure 4. The design of these menu commands is influenced by the organisation of the scientific concepts into the Ecolab I curriculum, hence the arrow between boxes 2 and 4.

The learner can interact with the Ecolab I simulation through the interface. Her interactions influence the learner model and the features of the software and activities that are made available through it. This is why the arrow linking the learner and interface is bi-directional, indicating that there is influence in both directions. The aim is that the learner's knowledge and understanding will be influenced through these interactions and that she will understand more. The arrow between boxes 3 and 4 is also bi-directional, to show that there is influence in both directions. The commands available through the interface are influenced by the underlying resources of the software and the availability of these in turn is influenced by the learner model, which is itself influenced by the learner's interactions through the interface.

In the Ecolab I software the system also plays the role of the MAP through its selection of assistance both in terms of the different levels of help made available to ensure that the learner can complete the actions she selects and in terms of the level of difficulty of the activity that is offered to the learner. The software makes decisions about this assistance based upon the model it maintains of the learner as she interacts with the system.

All these inter-linked elements represent the elements of the software context with which the learner can interact in the Ecolab I example. Of course the learner's interactions will take place within a particular physical location and will involve interactions with various other people and artefacts outside the software system. This wider environment will of course also influence the nature of the interactions that a learner has with the Ecolab I software. However, if we consider the software alone, then the Ecolab I could scaffold a learner to an increased understanding of some of the concepts of food web ecology through marshalling for the benefit of that learner the resources of a simulated laboratory environment to best meet her needs.

The extended Ecolab II software

Findings from the Ecolab I evaluation demonstrated that offering learners a combination of challenging activities and appropriate support could improve test scores, which may indicate learning. A further important finding from the Ecolab I evaluation was that the increased sophistication within the learner model did not result in more effective learning interactions for all learners. Help-seeking behaviour became an important factor and I wanted to explore how this aspect of metacognitive awareness might be scaffolded through the software. My aim for Ecolab II was to develop an environment that could provide metacognitive support to help learners improve their help-seeking and task-selection skills and, through this, their performance at learning about food chains and webs.

Metacognitive learner modelling and scaffolding

In addition to the different levels of help that Ecolab I offered learners when they were trying to complete actions within their simulation, Ecolab II offered learners:

1   Feedback on their progress through the rule nodes in the Ecolab II curriculum via a *progress* button that was added to the interface;
2   Additional help at four points during their interactions with Ecolab II:

   a   when the learner selects what he is going to learn about
   b   when the learner decides what level of challenge to choose
   c   when the learner needs help at the domain level
   d   during interactions, as a reminder to use the *progress* button.

The help at points 2 a–c above was available in three levels. For example, at point 2c, when a learner needs to select help at the domain level the following hints about using that help were available:

   Level 1   Don't forget that the Ecolab can help you
   Level 2   Why not ask for some **more/less** help (the system model of the learners is used to select either **more** or **less** help)
   Level 3   Try Level **X** help (where **X** is the level of help as indicated by the system's model of the learner)

In order for the Ecolab II software to be able to offer this type of assistance, additions were made to the learner model to encompass information about the learner's use of the metacognitive scaffolding hints and his performance with the Ecolab activities. This information was used to decide upon the level of the next metacognitive prompt to be offered to the learner and to make recommendations to the learner about how much domain level help to request.

Learning with Ecolab II

In an evaluation of the Ecolab II software with 32 children aged 9 to 11 years we measured children's learning using the same paper pre-test and post-test as was used in the original Ecolab I evaluation study (Luckin and Hammerton, 2002). The children participating in this study increased their scores between pre- and post-test. However, in this evaluation the relationship between the learning gains made and ability was particularly interesting and indicated that that children of low ability demonstrated greater proportional learning gains with Ecolab II, see Figure 5.

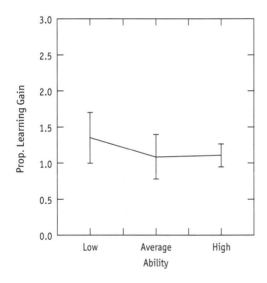

Figure 5 Proportional learning gains for children using Ecolab II

In the Ecolab I evaluation the extent to which learners had received assistance from the system in the form of the graded levels of help with actions and the Activity Differentiation of the activities they completed was related to their learning gains. This was true for Ecolab II also: a high percentage of the children with above average learning gains used a high level and an above average amount of system assistance:

- 73 per cent used a high level of system *help* and/or a high level of Activity Differentiation and 82 per cent used an above average amount of help and/or an above average amount of Activity Differentiation;
- 64 per cent used Ecolab I software in more than one phase of relationship *complexity* in combination with the use of above average quantities and qualities of system assistance.

Summary

The Ecolab I software demonstrated that software could be used to offer learners a variety of different types of assistance that could be described as the ZAA of the system. It also demonstrated that learners needed guidance to select the most appropriate quantities and qualities of assistance: in other words they needed support to construct the ZPA that met their needs. Ecolab II built on these findings and tried to support learners to be better at seeking appropriate help and building this ZPA. It demonstrated that it is possible to scaffold learners to select appropriately challenging tasks and suitable quantities and qualities of help. The resources that make up the ZAA of the Ecolab II software were very similar to those found in the Ecolab I software, with the addition of metacognitive help and an adapted role for the software as MAP. The Ecolab I software context depicted in Figure 4 has been adapted for Ecolab II and is illustrated in Figure 6. A key point to highlight is that Ecolab II explored the way in which help-seeking behaviour could be scaffolded.

In a world where there is an increased proliferation of possible resources that are accessible in so many different ways and that are subject to ongoing development and change, help-seeking is an increasingly important skill. Modelling a learner's interactions within a closed software environment, such as that offered by the Ecolab I and II, is relatively straightforward. When at least some of the resources whose use is to be scaffolded are outside the confines of the software, however, the situation is far more complex.

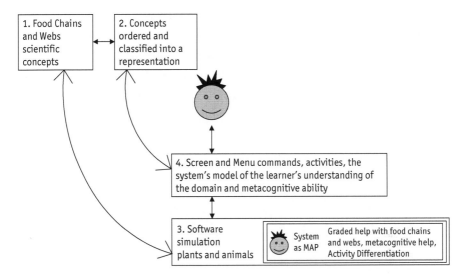

Figure 6 The elements in the Ecolab II software context

Looking outside the software

Several other projects offered me the opportunity to explore the growing variety of interactions that occur outside the confines of the single user and the software application: interactions between other resources in the learner's environment with, through and around the learner and the technology. These are interactions that could form part of the learner's ZPA and interactions that might therefore be of interest to any person or technology playing the role of the MAP.

The Riddles project introduced the Separate Control Of Shared Space (SCOSS) interface (Kerawalla *et al.*, 2008) and illustrated that its design could influence the manner in which the resources provided by software were made available to pairs of learners. The SCOSS interface differed from a single-user interface in the manner in which it gave each child (aged 7 to 9 years) in a pair simultaneous but separate control of their own area of the computer screen. Each child had her own mouse that she could use to manipulate screen elements in her own area of the screen and *only* her own area of the screen.

15

Each child could therefore engage with the particular resources provided by the software, but could not interfere with the resources being used by her partner. The interface design also influenced the learners' interactions with resources outside the software, namely their partners. It provided support for learners to collaborate but, without further scaffolding, the interface alone could not ensure that learners did collaborate nor could it influence the quality of this collaboration. Figure 7 illustrates the elements that made up the learning context for learners using Riddles project software called WordCat, which engaged pairs of children in a word categorisation task.

The CACHET project (Luckin *et al.*, 2003; Plowman and Luckin, 2004) explored the potential of commercially produced digital toys for learning with 4- to 6-year-old children at home, in after-school clubs and in a school. The children who used the interactive toys and accompanying software demonstrated the way in which the design of the interface to the software could influence the nature of the interactions the learner had with resources outside the confines of the software itself. When the toy was available as an interface to the

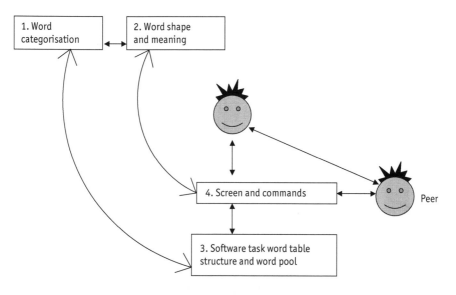

Figure 7 The elements of the Riddles WordCat software context

software (instead of an on-screen toy icon to be clicked with the mouse) there was increased interaction between the learner and the people available to help the learner. This study also illustrated the use of multiple interfaces to a single software application: the toy and the mouse. These multiple interfaces could enable each learner from a pair to interact with the resources of the software independently of each other and therefore, as in the case of the SCOSS interface, could influence a learner's interactions both with the software resources and with another learner if working other than alone. Figure 8 illustrates the elements that made up the learning context for learners in the CACHET project.

These studies made an important contribution to the Ecology of Resources model of context (Luckin, 2008). They illustrated that the design of technology can influence a learner's interactions with the resources in her environment beyond those provided solely by the software. They also suggested that, to an extent at least, we can also model these interactions as well as those between learners and the resources provided by the software. This highlighted the possibility that technology can have a role in supporting learning interactions across a range of resources and that as designers we need to understand more about the nature of these interactions and the way in which we might model them.

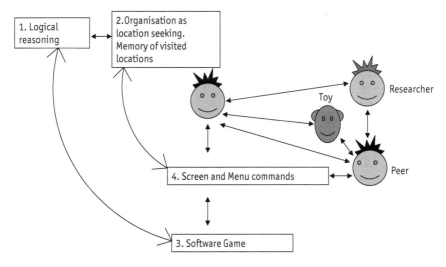

Figure 8 The elements of the Cachet context

17

The Homework project

In the final example I want to present here, I discuss the Homework project and the associated HOMEWORK software (Luckin *et al.*, 2006). This project explored how technology could be used with 5- to 6-year-old children to support their interactions with a variety of other people and a variety of other resources across a range of locations. The project was a collaboration between academics, film producers and broadcasters (Open Mind Productions and Channel 4 Learning), parents, teachers and children. It was based on an earlier version of the Ecology of Resources model called the Broadband Learner Model (Luckin and du Boulay, 2001). The focus for this Broadband Learner Model was also on modelling the learner and her interactions. The aim was to build a model of the learner's interactions that could take into account her interactions across multiple locations and with multiple other participants. The design of this multi-faceted Broadband Learner Model was also to be used as the template for descriptions of the resources that made up the subject domain knowledge of the learning interaction. These resources included multiple media (such as text, audio and video) about particular areas of the primary maths curriculum, along with information about the resources that were available to help the learner. These help resources included other people as well as hints and tips within the content resources themselves.

The HOMEWORK system was an interactive maths education system for children aged 5 to 7 years that used a combination of interactive whiteboard, tablet PC technology and some bespoke software. This software consisted of lesson planning, classroom control and home use components. The system contained a rich set of multimedia and associated interactive numeracy resources. Teachers used the software to link these resources together into lesson plans. In the classroom, the interactive whiteboard was used for whole-class activities and each child also had his own tablet PC for individual and small-group activities. The teacher could control the classroom activity from her own tablet PC and could allocate new activities or send messages to individuals or groups of children in real time. When planning each lesson the teacher could also decide upon homework activities and allocate them to individual children's tablets as appropriate. After school, the children took their tablet PC home with them and used it at home or elsewhere, individually or with parents. At home, in addition to homework activity set by the teacher, the tablet provided access to the resources used in class that day and in previous sessions (irrespective of whether the child was actually in school or not) and information for parents about the learning objectives to which these activities related. There were also links to other relevant fun activities, and a messaging system to support parent and teacher communication. Figure 9 illustrates the use of the HOMEWORK system in the school classroom and at home and Figure 10 illustrates the tablet PC interface seen by the children and their families when the tablet was outside the classroom.

Figure 9 HOMEWORK in use in the classroom and at home

The HOMEWORK system at school

The system was used for three hour-long maths lessons per week. The teacher would use the lesson-planning features of the system to plan each session. She would select the content she wanted the class, small groups or individual children to use. The resources associated with this content could then be allocated to the interactive whiteboard or the children's tablet PCs as appropriate. The teacher could also allocate homework activities to the tablets for each child. The interface that the HOMEWORK system offered the teacher to support lesson planning is illustrated in Figure 11. The classroom lessons usually consisted of

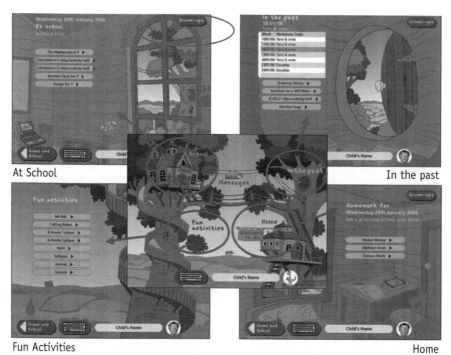

At School

In the past

Fun Activities

Home

Figure 10 The HOMEWORK system home interface

an initial session with the whole class sitting on the floor around the interactive whiteboard. In this session the children watched a short 'Number Crew' video together and completed some interactive activities as directed by the teacher and with individual children being called to the whiteboard to complete a particular action. After this children would go to their individual seats and use their tablet PCs to complete the activities that had been pre-selected for them by the teacher in advance of the lesson. The teacher could take control of one, some, or all of the tablet PCs if she wanted to send a particular message to members of her class.

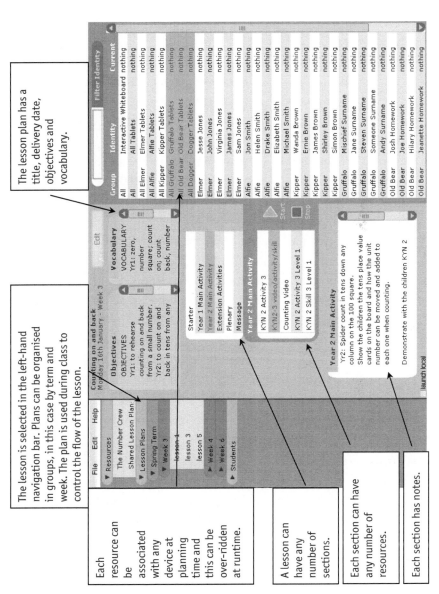

The lesson is selected in the left-hand navigation bar. Plans can be organised in groups, in this case by term and week. The plan is used during class to control the flow of the lesson.

The lesson plan has a title, delivery date, objectives and vocabulary.

Each resource can be associated with any device at planning time and this can be over-ridden at runtime.

A lesson can have any number of sections.

Each section can have any number of resources.

Each section has notes.

Figure 11 The HOMEWORK lesson planning interface for teachers

21

How the HOMEWORK system was used

The HOMEWORK system was developed incrementally and iteratively, through working with parents, teachers and learners using a participatory design approach. Evaluations of the HOMEWORK system with classes of children aged 5 to 7 years involved the collection of multiple data sources, including logs maintained by the system, diaries maintained by the parents, interviews with parents, and questionnaires completed by parents. The details of the study design, data sources and system version are presented in Luckin *et al.*, 2006.

During an evaluation of the Homework system in 2005, log data collected from 16 tablets over the week from 29 April to 5 May 2005 revealed that the average home session length was 31 minutes 13 seconds and that the average number of times the tablet PC was used at home was four. Interestingly this week included a bank holiday (2 May 2005) and nine out of the 16 tablets were used on that day. Diaries reveal that the most common time for the tablet to be used was weekday evenings, with a total of 79 uses recorded at this time. The next most common time was straight after school during the week (47 times), then during the day at weekends (or bank holidays) (38 times), then weekend evenings (17 times) and finally before school during the week (three times). The cut-off time between day and evening was 5.30 p.m. and early weekend morning means before 8 a.m.

These diaries also indicate that during evaluations in both 2005 and 2006 the system was most often used at a table located in a communal space such as a lounge, dining room or kitchen, followed by the bedroom and infrequently in a car or somewhere else. The nature of the tablet PC technology meant that the HOMEWORK system could be used in a wide variety of locations and in a range of ways. The data illustrates that the system was certainly used across a variety of locations. The occasions when this involved a location outside the house were not great, but the parental diary data illustrates both the potential afforded by this approach and the instances when this potential was fulfilled. For example:

> We'd just have a piano lesson and then he just does it, while his sister was having her half hour piano lesson he's on the computer in the car

waiting, it's brilliant – he would not do that if it was paper . . . I found that really useful, and his sister has tutoring on Friday evening for an hour, and he takes his PC. Before that it was a nightmare, but it was very easy just to whack out his tablet PC.

(A parent comment in a 2005 study interview)

The diaries also reflect that Mum was the person who most frequently helped children with their tablet activities, with Dad, siblings and other family members being the next most frequent helpers. The 'history' facility enabled families to view any activity and re-run any media that the children had used on their tablet PCs either at school or at home. This feature was intended to support parents who had asked to know more about what their children had done at school and to be able to follow their child's activities over time. Discussions in interviews and focus groups with parents reveal that the use of this history facility was family specific and often depended upon parents' perceived need for it: if their child was finding something particularly difficult, for example. There is also evidence in comments made by parents that the use of the history facility might be developed through increased familiarity:

I think if [the tablet] was to become part of the homework routine then we probably would get into the habit of reviewing work that's been done at school [using the history], get the hang of it ourselves, feel confident about it and then try and help [child's name] with her homework.

(A parent comment in a 2005 study interview)

The HOMEWORK system supporting families to support their child's learning

In 2006, parents could access information that had been specially created for them by pressing the 'grown-ups' button on the interface as illustrated in Figure 12.

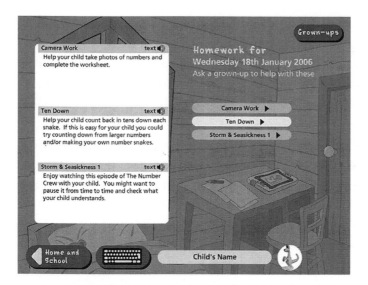

Figure 12 Help provided through the 'grown-ups' button

This button offered them information about the objectives of the activity, the vocabulary used and suggestions about how parents might help their child. Once the button had been selected, 'grown-ups' information was displayed until the button was switched off. In the evaluation study conducted in 2006 16 out of 26 parents were still using the 'grown-ups' facility at the end of the study on average once or twice during the final week, and the length of time for which the information was available for them to use during an activity had settled at just over 3 minutes. This comment from a parent illustrates the way that she used this feature.

> The story in the Number Crew video was great and we spoke about counting on afterwards as suggested in the 'grown-ups' information.
>
> (A parent comment in a 2006 study diary)

The impact of the HOMEWORK system on learning

There was evidence of learning gains during the time the HOMEWORK system was in use. In 2006, these gains can be seen in the changes in the pre-test and post-test scores recorded for students. The mean scores for the youngest children (aged 5–6) increased by 16.99 per cent and for the older children (aged 6–7) by 25.78 per cent. In addition to these test scores, comments made by parents in the diaries they maintained and during interviews also suggest that children's learning may have benefited during the Homework project studies. For example:

> I think he's much keener to do numeracy homework. I think we got very bored with the paper homework – it was just a bit flat and it was very basic and it wasn't very long and involved. He's spent a lot longer actually doing homework on this, probably because of the other skills levels and activities within the activities you can do. So he's spent much more time on it, which I would conclude means that he's practised and used his maths more.
>
> (A parent comment in a 2005 study interview)

In the interviews with the class teachers there are reports that reflect their belief that children are learning with their use of the HOMEWORK system. For example:

> I've certainly noticed people like [child's name]. She seems a lot more confident with her mental arithmetic. I don't know if that's as a result of using the tablet at home and in school or whether Mum's been doing extra things with her, I'm not sure.
>
> (A teacher comment from 2005 interview)

Finally, evidence of changes in learner behaviour can be found in the parental responses to a telephone questionnaire. This questionnaire was focused specifically on the children's completion of numeracy homework rather than their use of the HOMEWORK system in general; it nevertheless illustrates some interesting changes. The change most commonly reported by parents was that their child was doing numeracy homework without the parent asking and that their child was doing more than the minimum numeracy homework.

The data discussed so far is useful and suggests that the approach adopted by the Homework project team was successful in supporting young children's learning of maths in and out of school. It offers evidence that the manner in which the technology was used was appropriate for the families involved, that it integrated well with the out-of-school environment and that it enabled family members to feel better informed and better able to get involved with their child's education. However, the detail of what might account for these changes is unclear.

Family case studies

To explore more about the nature of the way in which the system may have supported learning and about the range of interactions that the HOMEWORK system was able to support I discuss excerpts from a family's use of the system in more depth. This narrative is constructed from the data logged by the Homework tablets and the entries made in the diary maintained by the family. The timings for the length spent on activities are to the nearest minute rounded down.

Alison's story

This excerpt is taken from a narrative about Alison and her family and the way that they used the HOMEWORK system in 2005. Alison is 6 years old and she has a sister called Catherine, and another sister called Elizabeth. Alison and her sisters live with Mum and Dad.

Once again the Homework tablets come home for the weekend on 29 April. Alison has friends visiting and on Saturday afternoon she shows them her Homework tablet. She shows them some of the videos, games and exercises. They open up the camera, play InkBall, and write in Windows Journal. Later that same day at about 6.50 p.m. Alison and Dad use the camera in the garden. Alison also spends 3 to 4 minutes completing some Number Crew calculations, watching a Number Crew video and opening her completed Skill 5 homework activity.

. . .

Later this evening at around 8.15 pm Alison does one of the homework activities in her bedroom on the bed with Dad. Alison does the 'Ten Thing Bowling' activity [as illustrated in Figure 13], Alison then does level 2 of the Skill 5 homework activity for about 5 minutes and finishes this session by watching some Number Crew videos with Dad.

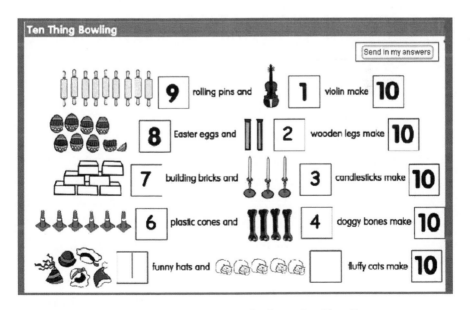

Figure 13 Homework activity: 'Ten Thing Bowling' completed by Alison

On Wednesday 4 May the Homework tablet comes home again and there are some new homework activities: '10p in different ways', 'Double Ice Creams' and 'Numbers in your home', which uses the tablet camera. Alison spends just over 35 minutes at about 6 p.m. working at the lounge table with Elizabeth and Mum. They begin with the '10p in different ways' homework sheet, which takes about 10 minutes. They then move onto the 'Numbers in your home' homework activity and they both spend about 15 minutes doing this. Mum says Alison's camera worked well at capturing the family dartboard and that they managed to use the touchpad fine. Alison finishes her session at about 6.40pm with a couple of minutes playing InkBall.

. . .

The start of a new week on Monday 9 May brings some new topics for Alison to learn. This week at school they study the time, the days of the week and the seasons. Alison works on her bed with Mum for about 25 minutes starting at about 8 p.m. They look at 'Number Crew Solving Problems' videos that the girls love and they both sing and bop along to them. There are some problems accessing the third homework activity so they look at some other Number Crew activities and Alison spends a couple of minutes working on Activity 8 at level 1.

. . .

On Thursday Alison takes her tablet home for the final time. Alison uses her tablet with her Mum and Elizabeth at about 5.15 p.m. while they watch Catherine take part in a karate lesson, so they use the headphones. Alison spends a few minutes writing in the Journal and they then watch two videos and complete Activities 8 and 6 before watching another video and stopping at 5.50 p.m.

Alison's story, along with those for other children offers an unusual and valuable insight into technology use out of school. I present excerpts here to illustrate what it can tell us about the interactions that make up Alison's learning context, rather than as an evaluation of the Homework project itself.

Narratives such as this provide interesting information about the ways in which the design of the system might be further improved. Alison makes use of the flexibility offered by the technology and uses her Homework tablet in a variety of locations, including the lounge, her bedroom, the garden and at her sister's karate club. She works on the floor, sofa, at a table or on her bed and at many different times throughout the day from just after 8 a.m. in the morning until after 9 p.m. at night. She can make the choices about when and where to work on her numeracy within the constraints negotiated with her family. Sometimes she works on an activity for a minute or two and on other occasions for 25 minutes. The Homework tablet is often used on more than one occasion in a day and for sessions of up to 40 minutes. Alison works on the homework activities set by Miss Green, but does much more besides these and clearly enjoys herself, provided that the technology is working properly. She is able to choose what she wants to work on, she can show it to her friends and other family members and in so doing behave independently. The numeracy activities sometimes offer Alison the opportunity to record information about her life outside school and she can also use the camera to capture information for numeracy activities about her home.

The whole family gets involved with the numeracy activities available through the Homework tablet. Mum, Dad and sisters all work with Alison during the study. They can do this in a way that fits with family life. Mum reports that she has an increased awareness of the numeracy that Alison is working on at school. Mum also reports that Alison's interest in numeracy has increased and that she has enjoyed the activities.

The More Able Partner role and personalisation

In a situation such as that described by the Homework case studies, it is clear that in the out-of-school environment alone there may be multiple people who play the role of the MAP at different points during the learner's interactions. Likewise in the school environment there will be the teacher, classroom assistant, peers, other teachers and parent helpers, each of whom may also play the role of the MAP at different points in time. The HOMEWORK system was designed to support both the child learning and also the people playing the role of her MAP. It also had a role to play in the negotiation of the learner's ZPA with and between those playing the role of her MAP, through, for example, the provision of information for parents and for teachers about what each had done with the learner at home and at school. The data gained from the Homework project is helpful in providing a starting place for working out how best the technology can support this negotiation. For example, the information for grown-ups supports communication between teacher and parent to engender continuity of language in the way that the activities are discussed with the learner; also the ability to replay and review completed activities enables each person acting as the learner's MAP to see what the child has done when working alone or with another. In addition to supporting others playing the role of a MAP, the system itself had a role to play as a MAP through the carefully designed scaffolding provided for learners.

The Homework project also highlighted some interesting issues about the personalisation of learning. For example, it highlighted the fact that the experience that a learner has when using a particular piece of content is part of its personalisation for that learner. So whilst two learners may both watch the same video clip or complete the same worksheet in their homes, their experience of this will be different because of the interactions that surround their experience, such as the conversations they have with their sibling about the video clip or the comment that Mum makes whilst they are completing the worksheet. This means that no assumptions can be made about content that works well in school working equally well or in the same way when it is used outside the school.

The Ecology of Resources model of context

My aim in exploring all the projects discussed here is to extract the findings from these projects that have influenced the construction of the Ecology of Resources model of context. The Homework project example explored the most complex situation with respect to the learner, with respect to those who can act in the role of the MAP and with respect to the role that technology can play in these interactions. This expanded our knowledge about the range of context elements with which the learner could interact. Interactions between a learner and resources outside the classroom could be recorded and analysed. The findings that emerge illustrate the importance of using technology to offer conceptual coherence between these multiple interactions. In order to increase the coherence of the conceptual interactions that a learner experiences as she learns with technology support, the technology and the role for which it is designed need to support building coherence between the multiple interactions within a learner's context. In order to design technology to meet this need the model that grounds the design framework on which it is based must map out the type of elements that a learner is likely to interact with and must consider how to support coherence between the interactions that occur between these different elements. This is the aim of the Ecology of Resources model of context.

The Ecology of Resources context elements

The Ecology of Resources model maps out the different types of element that might offer interactive possibilities for a particular learner and it considers the interactions that can exist between these element types. See Figure 14 for an illustration of these elements.

The model has the learner at its centre and the learner interacts with each category of element. The concepts that make up the knowledge and skills that are the subject of the learning are represented by the 'Knowledge' label. It is important to stress that this label encompasses skills, as well as knowledge of scientific concepts. A second category is that represented by the 'Resources' label. These are all the various resources that might help the learner to learn and include books, pens and paper, technology and other people, some of whom know more about the knowledge or skill to be learnt than the learner. The last category of context element is that represented by the 'Environment' label. This is the location and surrounding environment with which the learner interacts. This might be a school classroom, a park or a place of work. In many instances

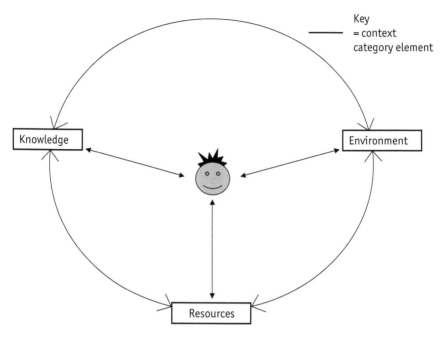

Figure 14 The context elements in the Ecology of Resources

a relationship already exists between these three types of contextual element: knowledge (and skills), resources (human and artefact) and environment. Hence the categories of element surrounding the learner and with which they interact are joined together. In order to support learning the relationships between the different types of element with which the learner interacts need to be understood and can be used to build coherence into the interactions experienced by the learner.

The Ecology of Resources filter elements

However, a learner's interactions with the elements that make up her context are often filtered by the actions of others rather than experienced directly by the learner. For example, the knowledge or skills that are to be learnt are usually filtered through some kind of organisation or curriculum that has been the subject of a process of validation by other members of the learner's society. This filter is stronger for subjects such as maths and other formal educational disciplines than for more grounded skills such as motor mechanics. However, even with skills-based subjects there is still, to some extent at least, formalisation of what is recognised as the accepted view about the nature and components of the skill that need to be mastered. The resources that may be available to the learner are also organised in some way. I use the word 'Administration' to describe this organisation. This administration forms a filter in terms of a learner's access to at least some of the resources that might be available to help her learn. Finally, a learner's access to the environment is mediated by that environment's organisation. As in the case of knowledge, this organisation is more obvious in formal settings such as schools where timetables and regulations have a strong influence on the ways in which learners interact with their environment. These filter elements have been added to the model illustrated in Figure 15.

In the same way that there may already exist relationships between the different context elements, there may also exist a relationship between these filter elements. For example, the organisation of the numeracy curriculum in the Homework project influenced the teacher's choice of resource for her lesson plan and the nature of the technology that was to be used by learners: the interactive whiteboard or the tablet PC. The layout of the classroom was also influenced by the nature of the resources being used, needing a floor space near the interactive whiteboard large enough to seat the whole class, for example. These relationships are illustrated through the connections between the filters in Figure 15. Once again, the coherence of the learner's experience can be enhanced through careful consideration of the existing relationships between the filters and between the individual context elements and their associated filters.

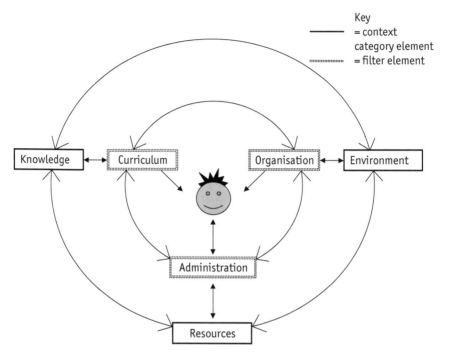

Figure 15 The context elements and their filters

Relationships in the Ecology of Resources

The Ecology of Resources model represents the learner holistically with respect to the interactions that make up their context. The model draws attention to different categories of element and identifies the existence of filter elements to highlight where there may be perturbations, which can be either negative or positive, in the learner's interactions. However, it is the relationships and inter-actions between elements and between learner and elements that are of real interest. It is therefore to these that I pay particular attention here. These relationships are complex. Each category of element and therefore each element in that category is related to each of the other elements as well as to the learner. As indicated in the early discussions of the Ecolab software context and illus-trated in Figure 4, the nature of the relationship represented by the arrows in the Ecology of Resources model is one of influence. One element influences a second and that second element is influenced by the first.

There are also relationships and interactions between the elements that are part of the same category of element. These relationships are of four types:

- influence relationships as already discussed
- component relationships in which one element is part of another
- typology relationships in which one element is a type of another
- social relationships such as that between family members, friends or communities.

The Homework project as an Ecology of Resources

The Homework project can provide an example of how the Ecology of Resources model can be used. An initial representation of the different context elements for learners in the Homework project is illustrated in Table 1. This is not an exhaustive representation. The relationships between the elements of the same category can be seen to be 'constituent/part of', 'type of' or 'social/family'; there are no examples of 'influences' relationships within the elements in this particular example. A subset of this model is illustrated in Figure 16.

In Table 1 the context elements of the outer ring of the graphical representation of the model are in the left-hand column of the table and the filter elements from the inner ring of the graphical representation are in the right-hand column. As explained earlier, the relationship between the different context elements of the model is one of influence. For example, starting with the elements in the left-hand column of Table 1, the numeracy concepts being studied influence the resources that are selected and the manner in which the physical environment of the classroom will be used. The resource administration by the teacher in her selection of resources is influenced by the curriculum and will influence the way that she organises the lesson. The school organisation constrains the length of that lesson and therefore the length of time that numeracy can be learnt at school.

Context element		Filter element
Knowledge		*Curriculum*
Numeracy		UK National Curriculum at KS 1 and 2
The *constituent* parts of numeracy knowledge include the following:	Influences	The *constituent* parts of this curriculum include the following:
counting addition subtraction.		adding 2 numbers to equal 10 adding or subtracting the numbers 9 and 11.
Influences		Influences
Resources		*Administration*
The *types* of resource include:		
Human resources *Types* might include friends and family. *Types* of family might include mum, dad, sibling.		The *types* of administration of human resources include family and *social* norms and relationships.
Physical resources *Types* include paper, pen and Homework Tablet PC. *Constituent* parts of the Tablet PC include: battery, charger, screen.	Influences	The *types* of administration of physical resources include classroom and/or home systems. In the class the teacher will constrain access; at home parents may do likewise.
Digital resources *Types* include Number Crew		The *types* of administration of digital resources include the

activities, Number Crew videos, Homework activities, journal, pictures, Paint and InkBall.		software on the Tablet, the selection of content made by the design team, and the selection of content made by the teacher for a particular learner.
Influences		Influences
Environment The *constituent* parts of the environment may include: School The *constituent* parts of the school may include: classroom, library, playground. Home The *constituent* parts of the home may include: rooms, garden, objects. The different *types* of room may include dining room, lounge, bedroom. Between home and school The different *types* of environment may include social club, sports ground, library.	Influences	*Organisation* The *types* of constraints on the school environment may include timetable, school rules, room allocation. The *types* of constraints on the home environment may include the 'rules' of the household, such as bed times and where work can be done. The *types* of constraints on the 'between home and school' environments may include the 'rules' of a club or the library, and health and safety regulations for sports.

Table 1 Homework Ecology of Resources example

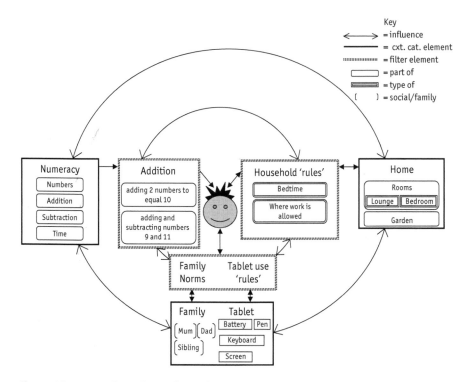

Figure 16 Excerpt from the Ecology of Resources model for Homework

The relationship between elements in different columns of Table 1 (and there-fore in different rings of the graphical representation) is also one of influence, in particular the constraining influence of the filters on the availability of a particular context element. So, for example, the relationship between knowledge and curriculum is one in which the curriculum filter element con-strains the nature of the knowledge offered to the learner. In return, the activity of creating curricula and of organising knowledge may influence changes in the underlying knowledge concepts. However, the relationship between knowledge and curriculum is mutual in principle. In a similar manner the administration filter constrains access to the resources and the organisation filter constrains access to the environment. Again in principle the relationship is mutual. This constraint can sometimes be positive: for example the fact that the learner does not have completely free access to all classroom resources may prevent her from being overwhelmed. These constraints can also be negative: for example if the school timetable constrains the amount of time available for numeracy too much. It is important to consider the filter elements when assessing how available to the learner the resources in the Ecology of Resources really are, and what influence the learner may have on her interactions with the elements of her context. In Figure 16 I have linked the learner to all context elements via the filter elements and have used a bi-directional arrow for the family and tablet resources and the home environment, but a uni-directional arrow for numeracy knowledge. I have used a uni-directional arrow for this relationship in this example to indicate that for the most part learners have no influence on the nature of either the knowledge or its organisation into a curriculum. In principle, and at advanced levels of learning such as when studying for a PhD, it is possible that the learner may influence both the knowledge concepts and their organisation into curricula. However, that is not the case for the Homework learner.

The learner's culture and history

All of the elements in any Ecology of Resources bring with them a history that defines them and the part they play in the wider cultural and political system. Likewise, the individual at the centre of the Ecology of Resources has her own history of experience that impacts upon her interactions with each of the elements in the Ecology. This wider history and culture is represented in Figure 17 by the shaded areas that surround each of the pairs of elements and the learner at the centre. The existence and the importance of this wider cultural perspective can be addressed through the use of participatory methods to develop effective technologies. It also prompts the need for a detailed discussion, beyond the scope of this lecture, of the way in which the Ecology of Resources model can be used as the basis for learning modelling activity. The Ecology of Resources model is also the lynchpin for a design framework.

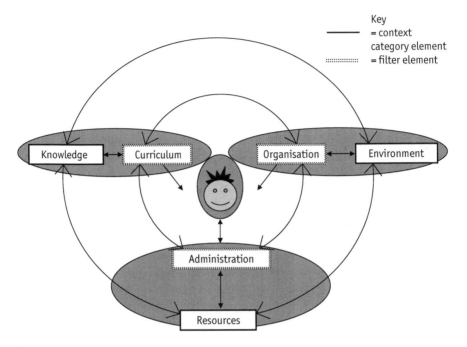

Figure 17 The Ecology of Resources

Conclusions and future implications

In the last section of this lecture I want to expand upon each of three pairs of key issues that emerge from the previous discussion and that relate to the learner's wider social, political and cultural setting and highlight the implications of the Ecology of Resources for some current aspects of this wider educational agenda. From each key issue pair I extract a contemporary illusion that needs to be addressed.

Key issues pair 1

First, I have illustrated that software can be used to offer learners a variety of different types of assistance that can be described as a Zone of Available Assistance, and that it can offer guidance to learners to help them select the most appropriate quantities and qualities of assistance to construct the Zone of

Proximal Adjustment that meets their needs. Two key issues that I highlight here are:

- The increasing importance of metacognitive or Higher Order Thinking skills (HOTs) in an increasingly connected and resource-rich world;
- The importance of the role of the More Able Partner. If learners need help to select appropriately from within the resources available within a single piece of software, it seems reasonable to believe that they will also need help to select from amongst resources available more widely in the world.

The knowledge illusion

The current popularity amongst learners for the production and publication of their own material, if combined with open-content and open-source initiatives, offers the tools for new learning opportunities. However, learners often lack the skills to take best advantage of these tools to support their learning. In particular they lack the HOTs they need to make decisions about the reliability of information and justification of knowledge (Luckin *et al.*, 2008). This in turn means that there is a crucial role for the MAP, maybe a teacher, who must understand the deep levels of engagement that technologies such as Web 2.0 can provide and how these can be translated into a higher level of critical engagement with information and communications technologies. MAPs have a vitally important role in the realisation of the transformative power of technology, but this role is continually evolving and MAPs need support to operate effectively in a 'perpetual beta' world.

There are *implications* of key issues pair 1 for curriculum reform, teacher training and school leadership.

Key issues pair 2

Secondly, I have illustrated that both in and out of school there are multiple people who play the role of the MAP at different points during the learner's interactions and that their role can be supported and co-ordinated, provided the provision of 'conceptual bridging' is the focus of attention for the application of technology. I have also highlighted the fact that the experience that a learner has when using a particular piece of content is part of its personalisation for that learner. Two key issues that I highlight here are:

- The way in which the different elements in a learner's Ecology of Resources can be co-ordinated across time and space to support the construction of her ZPA;
- The contextual nature of personalising learning.

The technology illusion

The key challenge we now face is to develop ways in which learners can change the *operational* network of technologies, people, places and things into a *conceptual* network of understanding and knowledge creation. These are the twenty-first-century learning skills we need to foster. Technology in itself is not the answer; it is the way that people use technology and in turn how this usage then transforms their lives that is the answer. We have to move on from the stage of talking about the specifics of technologies such as Web 2.0, or Second Life, and realise that these simply represent the current evolutionary instantiation of our relationship to technology. The crucial educational transformation question of what we want education to be in the twenty-first century is that we want it to be about enabling people to identify, support and develop appropriate relationships between the elements in their Ecology of Resources.

There are *implications* of key issue pair 2 for the Universal Home Access initiative, for example. It is extremely important that we invest in offering all families the opportunities to engage in the type of learning we saw in Alison's story. But the key to success will be in the way in which learning is supported through the development of appropriate content and co-ordination of the different individuals who act as the learner's MAP.

Key issue pair 3

Thirdly, I have stated that in order to increase the coherence of the conceptual interactions that a learner experiences as she learns with technology support, the technology and the role for which it is designed need to support building coherence between the multiple interactions within a learner's context. I have presented the Ecology of Resources model of context as the basis for a design framework to support this enterprise. Two key issues that I highlight here are that:

- The Ecology of Resources model represents the learner holistically with respect to the interactions that make up their context;
- It is the relationships and interactions between the elements and between learner and elements that are most important.

The institution illusion

We need to open up the process through which understanding is gained and knowledge is constructed and to facilitate the development of context-based models as the organising principle for designing learning. This requires us to embrace the idea that a learner's context is made up from the combination of interactions a learner experiences across multiple physical spaces and times. Every person's context is individual to them and is the ultimate form of person-alisation of the world and of the elements of the world that can contribute to learning. As technologies increasingly enable these different elements to be linked together and offer learners increased opportunities to interact with these elements and with the manner in which they are linked, then learners can take greater agency in the creation of their learning contexts through a constant series of adjustments to this dynamic environment. This offers the opportunity for moving beyond the generation of content for learning by learners to the gener-ation of contexts for learning by learners. Institutions such as schools have a key place within this ecology of learning resources, but their importance is as much about how they enable learners to build links between their experiences outside the school as it is with the way that they support learning experiences within the school.

There are implications of key issue pair 3 for the Building Schools for the Future programme in a world where education will be based less around phys-ical spaces and more around individual learners and the resources with which they interact.

References

Cole, M. (2003) 'Vygotsky and context. Where did the connection come from and what difference does it make? *Proceedings of International Society for Theoretical Psychology Conference*. Istanbul, Turkey: Campus Press. Available online from http://lchc.ucsd.edu/People/MCole/lsvcontext.html (retrieved 6 December 2008).

Dey, A.K. (2001) 'Understanding and using context'. *Personal and Ubiquitous Computing Journal*, 5(1), 4–7.

Griffiths, A.K. and Grant, A.C. (1985) 'High school students' understanding of food webs'. *Journal of Research in Science Teaching*, 22(5), 421–36.

Kerawalla, L., Pearce, D., Yuill, N., Luckin, R. and Harris, A. (2008) '"I'm keeping those there, are you?" The role of a new user interface paradigm – Separate Control of Shared Space (SCOSS) – in the collaborative decision-making process'. *Computers and Education*, 50(1), 193–206.

Luckin, R. (1998) '"ECOLAB": Explorations in the Zone of Proximal Development'. DPhil thesis: CSRP Technical Report 486. School of Cognitive and Computing Sciences, University of Sussex.

Luckin, R. (2008) 'The learner centric ecology of resources: a framework for using technology to scaffold learning'. *Computers and Education*, 50(2), 449–62.

Luckin, R. and du Boulay, B. (1999) 'Ecolab: the development and evaluation of a Vygotskian design framework'. *International Journal of Artificial Intelligence and Education*, 10(2), 198–220.

Luckin, R. and du Boulay, B. (2001) 'Embedding AIED in ie-TV through Broadband User Modelling (BbUM)'. In J. Moore, W.L. Johnson and C.L. Redfield (eds), *Proceedings of 10th International Conference on Artificial Intelligence in Education: AI-ED in the Wired and Wireless Future*. Amsterdam: IOS Press, 322–33.

Luckin, R. and Hammerton, L. (2002) 'Getting to know me: helping learners understand their own learning needs through metacognitive scaffolding'. In S.A. Cerri, G. Gouarderes and F. Paranguaca (eds), *Intelligent Tutoring Systems*. Berlin: Springer-Verlag, 759–71.

Luckin, R., Connolly, D., Plowman, L. and Airey, S. (2003) 'With a little help from my friends: children's interactions with interactive toy technology'. *Journal of Computer Assisted Learning* (Special issue on Children and Technology), 19(2), 165–76.

Luckin, R., du Boulay, B., Underwood, J., Holmberg, J., Kerawalla, L., O'Connor, J., Smith, H. and Tunley, H. (2006) 'Designing educational systems fit for use: a case study in the application of human centred design for AIED'. *International Journal of Artificial Intelligence in Education*, 16, 353–80.

Luckin, R., Logan, K., Clark, W., Graber, R., Oliver, M. and Mee, A. (2008) *Learners' use of Web 2.0 Technologies in and out of School in Key Stages 3 and 4*. Coventry: Becta.

Lumpe, A.T. and Staver, J.R. (1995) 'Peer collaboration and concept development: learning about photosynthesis'. *Journal of Research in Science Teaching*, 32(1), 71–98.

Mercer, N. (1992) 'Culture, context and the construction of knowledge in the classroom'. In P. Light and G. Butterworth (eds), *Context and Cognition: Ways of learning and knowing*. Hillsdale, NJ: Erlbaum, 28–46.

Nardi, B.A. (ed.) (1996) *Context and Consciousness: Activity theory and human-computer interaction*. Cambridge, MA and London: MIT Press.

Plowman, L. and Luckin, R. (2004) 'Interactivity, interface and smart toys'. *IEEE Computer*, February, 98–100.

Rogers, Y. (2006) 'Moving on from Weiser's vision of calm computing: engaging UbiComp experiences'. In P. Dourish and A. Friday (eds), *Ubicomp 2006: Ubiquitous computing*. Conference proceedings. Berlin: Springer-Verlag, 404–21.

Vygotsky, L.S. (1978) *Mind in Society: The development of higher psychological processes*, trans. M. Cole, V. John-Steiner, S. Scribner and E. Souberman. Cambridge, MA: Harvard University Press.

Vygotsky, L.S. (1986) *Thought and Language*. Cambridge, MA: MIT Press.

Wood, D., Bruner, J.S. and Ross, G. (1976) 'The role of tutoring in problem solving'. *Journal of Child Psychology and Psychiatry*, 17(2), 89–100.

Wood, D.J., Wood, H.A. and Middleton, D.J. (1978) 'An experimental evaluation of four face-to-face teaching strategies'. *International Journal of Behavioral Development*, 1, 131–47.

Wood, D., Underwood, J. and Avis, P. (1999) 'Integrated learning systems in the classroom'. *Computers and Education*, 33(2/3), 9.